LISTEN FOR THE LORD

*God's Messages of Love,
Guidance and Inspiration*

Written by Helen Mallicoat

Hallmark Editions

Aug. 5, 85

Dear Kay,

I tried to call you today but didn't get an answer. We hope that's a good sign and that you are feeling much better.

Julie anne is coming on Thursday. We have to meet Pat about half way for both of us, at Geneva on the lake. Chuck & Pat plan to come next Wed and so does Faye & kids

Edited by Tina Hacker. Designed by Rick Cusick

Material in this book excerpted from *Things Seen and Heard* by Helen Mallicoat.

©1977, Hallmark Cards, Inc., Kansas City, Missouri.

Printed in the United States of America.

Standard Book Number: 87529-519-3.

Mom & Dad

Lane is coming on Friday, some of her class mates are having a picnic out at Pat & Norm Rifes. She has to go back home on Monday. I thought you would enjoy this little book. Love you much

Dear Reader:

For several years, God has been teaching me lessons and giving me advice through dreams, visions and direct conversations. He has been my Friend, Counselor, Physician, Teacher and Saviour. But the lessons God has taught me are not for my use alone. Just as His Words have helped and comforted me, I know they can help others as well. That is why I have written down His Words for everyone to share.

Together, we can all grow in understanding and love for God until all barriers are removed and we can constantly walk and talk with Him. When this happens, the walls of misunderstanding will be broken down between man and man, too. Then we shall truly be of one mind and one spirit.

With love,
Helen Mallicoat

I saw a man with flowing hair and robe. He was walking down a winding road. He held a child by each hand — a boy and a girl. The children were dressed in clean bright clothing, as if dressed for school.

I said, "What do I see? What does this mean?" They turned toward me. The Man was my Lord. He looked into my eyes, into my very being. The children and the road were gone, even myself. Only He was there. He filled ALL.

He spoke, "With all your learning, you know yet so very little."

Again I saw His face, now all tender compassion. He was saying, "But I shall remove the scales from your eyes. I shall cause you to see things as they really are. And I am removing stoppers from your ears. I am causing you to hear my voice. I shall tame your tongue and shall cause you to speak only my words." He was gone from my sight. I was never to be the same. I knew the promise was not to me only.

LIVING IN THE PRESENT

I was regretting the past and fearing the future. Suddenly my Teacher was speaking: "My name is I AM." He paused. I waited. He continued, "When you live in the past, with its mistakes and regrets, it is hard. I am not there. My name is not I WAS. When you live in the future, with its problems and fears, it is hard. I am not there. My name is not I WILL BE. When you live in this moment, it is not hard. I am HERE. My name is I AM."

OUR HELPER

Whenever I lose something or have a problem, I talk it over with my Friend. Always He tells me where or shows me the lost object. Often He gives me immediate solutions to my problems.

Only recently I was making jelly. While washing the containers, I dropped a small glass upside down in the garbage disposal. I could not get it out. I said, "Lord, you've always shown me simple ways to solve these little problems; but I can't see any simple way to get that glass out."

He answered me. It always surprises and delights me when He talks to me. "I'll show you, just wait." I began to rinse other jars and glasses. I let the water run into the disposal. Suddenly the disposal filled with water, the little glass floated, rose to the top and out into the sink! How simple, and how quickly He had kept His promise to me. I could feel Him smiling at my surprise and delight. Surely He is our True and Faithful loving Friend.

Often and always unexpectedly, my Master speaks to me. One night my mind rambled here and there. I could not control it. I grew weary with thinking — thinking round and round in circles. There were no answers, no solutions. Then came the voice of my Teacher, "This is the little lost sheep. It is always going astray." I thought about that remark. I agreed. It is our lost straying mind that gives us trouble. Again unexpectedly, He added, "But am I not faithful to search it out and bring it back to Myself?"

I was home. There were no questions. There were no wonderings or wanderings. Faith in His faithfulness is the answer and solution. In His faithfulness, He brings us faith.

Another time my mind was wandering to no seeming profit. I found myself speaking with great authority, "Mind, come back here and get into my head, and it is lying right here on my pillow." It was the voice of my Master speaking through me. Immediately my thoughts became reverent and rejoiceful, soon I was asleep. Since these two times, almost always, my mind is under control.

GOD'S PERFECT LOVE FOR US

I was thinking about the love of God for us and through us. He began to speak, "I love you with all My heart, with all My mind, with all My strength." Struck with awe at the magnitude of this statement, I waited in silence before Him. Finally He added, "I love your neighbor in the very same way." Knowing His love for me, knowing His love for my neighbor, now I can love my neighbor more perfectly also.

I AM WITH YOU ALWAYS

I had known the presence of the Lord continually for days. One day He did not make Himself known to me. That night I said, "Lord, I missed you today." He answered, "I've been with you all day. Why have you ignored Me?"

My son was going far away to make his home. As he left I said, "I'm so glad your Father and Elder Brother are going with you. Just don't ignore Them." He answered, "Mother, how can you ignore God?" I knew my son had gone a step farther than his mother.

LEARNING TO RELAX

It had been a long, fruitful, but tiring journey. Coming home, I became deathly ill. I was so tense that I thought my head would actually explode. My teen-age daughter was there when I arrived home. She massaged my head, neck and shoulders. I was desperate. I said to her, "Honey, what am I going to do?"

She answered calmly. "Mother, you're going to just let it hurt until it gets through." Suddenly I was well. All tension left. I was free and so very grateful to God! I had been too sick and weary to submit, so she had submitted for me.

The next morning as I awoke, the word 'SUBLAXATION' was saying itself within. I could not find the meaning in the dictionary. I found 'LAXATION' meant the ability to relax. I knew the Lord was telling me that my ability to relax was under par. More important, He was saying that He would teach me to relax more completely and perfectly. I have found Him true to His word.

THERE'S PLENTY OF TIME

One night I dreamed a confused dream. I was busy. I hurried, yet I couldn't accomplish anything. There were many people in the dream. I wanted to serve and please them all. I pleased none. I was displeased myself.

I awoke, still tired and confused. I knew I was to learn something from the dream. Later that day I sat resting. Suddenly my Teacher was saying, "I am not a slave driver. My yoke is easy. My burden is light." He waited for a long moment, then added, "There will NEVER be enough time, energy, inspiration to do all you want to do, all others want you to do and all I want you to do. BUT there will ALWAYS be plenty of time, energy and inspiration to do what I want you to do. What I want you to do is the only lasting, satisfying work. Wait for Me to instruct. I shall surely let you know."

I have found it so.

GOING FORWARD

I was dreaming. I was preparing food for a large number of people. I needed to go to the store. One of the men offered to take me. I'd purchased the item and was back in the car. My friend backed up to turn around. I was telling him something, when he stopped and said, "Well, here we are home." I said surprised, "Why I thought we were still going backward!"

He smiled and said, "Haven't you learned that there is never a going backward? There is always a going onward in the Plan of God." He laughed happily and added, "We always arrive at home, even when it seems we are going backward."

In my sleep my Teacher was saying, "The church buildings are full of stones — but they are living stones." (I saw, as it were, a rock pile. The stones were grey-black, dull. They were of various shapes and sizes. They were in a stationary pile.) My Teacher continued, "Now and then I pick one out, take it unto Myself to cut, polish and smooth it, to fit into a wall." (I saw a partially finished wall made of beautiful stones. They were of many colors. They were still of various shapes. They were all smooth.) My Teacher again spoke, "I am mortaring them together with LOVE, to make a permanent habitation for Myself."

In a dream, I was looking at a beautiful bright rainbow that went from horizon to horizon. I stood and marvelled and adored. Then the voice of my Friend was saying, "It doesn't go from horizon to horizon. That is only as far as you can see. It encircles the world."

Suddenly I saw the world and the rainbow encircling it all. I stood in awe and wonder. My Friend and Teacher added, "It is the Grace of God."

I awoke and continued to marvel. I knew that God's Grace is all that God is. He keeps watch over His creation constantly. Nothing can go wrong. His plan for His universe, and all it contains, shall be perfectly and completely fulfilled.

We had a new granddaughter. Her parents could not choose a name for her. Five days passed. I was going about my morning chores. Suddenly my Friend said, "Her name is Lori Carla." I was startled, and wondered if it was really God who had spoken to me.

Later the same morning the telephone rang. It was the other grandmother. She said, "They've finally named the baby. They're going to call her Lori Carla."

I was not surprised. I was thrilled. THEY had not named her. God had long ago. It was already Lori Carla. Now I know names — given names — are important; not titles plus last names, but given first names. God named me. He named you. He calls us by name.

I was dreaming. A friend and I were walking up a long hill. Suddenly it became smooth and glistening. At the top, we stepped into a beautiful garden. It was filled with flowering plants and shrubs everywhere. The tree we were standing under was also covered with blossoms. The branches came down near the ground and formed a sort of bower. I looked up toward the top. The farther I looked, the brighter and redder became the trumpet-shaped flowers. I was filled with glorious ecstasy. Then I remembered my friend and his recent trouble and I felt sorry that anyone in all the earth should be unhappy. I reached and touched my friend's shoulder and said, "I'm sorry." Then I knew he, too, had forgotten his troubles, for he asked, "About what?" I answered, "About all the troubles in the world." He said with tender sureness, "It's all right. Everything is all right." Then we continued on down a road toward home. I knew the 'home' was God.

The dream was over. The happiness remained. Several days passed. I became guilty that I should dwell in such happiness when many never in this life know such joy. Then Jesus was saying to me, "Accept this as a gift from Me." I thought about His statement for a minute, then He added, "Accept EVERYTHING as a gift from Me." I knew that everything that comes to us in our life is a gift from God, used for our good.

BREAD BAKING

I was dreaming. My Teacher was saying to me in the dream, "It is the sole duty and responsibility of My Spirit within you to bring you from 'the state of nothingness' to the understanding that nothing can separate you from the Love of God."

I returned to sleep. I dreamed I was in a daughter's house. Some friends were with me. My daughter was busy about the house. The children were making their sounds in the background. We sat in her living room. I was telling them about the dream and what my Teacher had told me. My daughter came and stood in the doorway. She said, "There is such a warm feeling in my house and a good smell. It is as if fresh made bread were baking in the oven." It was the Bread of Heaven — Jesus Christ making Himself known to us all.

The dream was ended. I awoke and knew that we are one bread. We feed and feed from one another.

I saw an orchard of small bushlike shrubs. The first rows were as black lifeless sticks. I knew it was their wintertime.

The next several rows were budding. I saw green leaves here and there. Spring had come. The next rows seemed to merge. They were thick with full green foliage. I saw a beautiful pinkish, yellowish white blossom here and there.

Then I saw the last rows filled with fruit. The fruit was only partially ripe. Some was green. The vision was gone. I felt a sadness. "Oh, Lord," I cried, "is there yet no ripe fruit anywhere?"

Again I saw the orchard. I saw it in all its stages. On a bush in the last row I saw, hidden under a cluster of leaves, a ripe fruit.

I reached and plucked the fruit. I held it in my hand. It felt cool and smooth. Its fragrance rose and blessed me. I could almost taste the sweet juiciness I knew it contained. It was almost round in shape —

not quite. It was a blend of colors — pink, pale green, yellow and white. I could see the faint lines beginning at the stem and meeting at the bottom. These were segments. I knew each of the segments were a fruit of the Spirit — Love, Joy, Peace, Patience, Gentleness, Goodness, Faith, Humility and Balance. I said, "There must be nine segments!"

I heard the Voice behind — the Voice of the Gardener: "No, there are only eight. The whole fruit is LOVE." It was harvesttime.

A GOOD FATHER

A grandson was living with us. He was gone this night. It was late. There was no way of finding where he was. I prayed. I worried. Finally my Teacher said, "I know where he is. He knows where he is, and you don't need to know." A joyous confidence came to me. How peace-giving it is to trust our children with their Father.

The incident happened several years ago. The grandson went through many trials. Our faith in our Father had to be renewed many times. Now he is married, the father of a beautiful little girl, and best of all he knows, loves and trusts God. Again God had proven He is a Good Father.

TRUSTING GOD

A certain problem in my life was worrying me. I was troubled. I could not forget it. I kept hearing the voice of my Friend saying, "Trust Me. Trust Me." I kept right on fretting and mulling it about in my mind. Hours passed — miserable hours. The Voice of my Friend became the Voice of my Master, "I said to trust Me! I know what I'm doing!" His command brought the ability to obey. Within a very short time the situation worked itself out, far beyond my fondest expectations. Now when troublesome situations arise I remember Him saying, "I KNOW what I'm doing."

I was questioned and was questioning about the so-called 'God-Head-Trinity'. The names Father, Son, Holy Ghost, Church whirled around in my head. Suddenly there was a calm, a stillness. I saw a beautiful young woman. Her hair was long, thick and dark. It flowed over her shoulders and down her back. Her eyes were soft, dark and deep. Her face was beautiful. Upon her lap was a beautiful, healthy, happy baby. He was nursing at her full breast. It was a perfect portrayal of peaceful completeness.

As I looked, I knew the mother was God and the breast was Christ. That which the baby was receiving was the unseen Spirit. It was the health-giving, warm, satisfying, comforting Essence of God.

The baby was humanity, held in the arms of God. God looked down on him with watchful, loving care. The baby was drawing all that was needed from God, but he was concerned only with the sweetness of the breast — Jesus, the Mediator between God and man. All is God. God is all. He is Love. He is enough.

ABIDING LOVE

A young man had had a real experience with God and had come to know and love Him. Yet there were times when it seemed it was not enough. Seemingly bad things were still happening. I wrestled within myself about these things. Finally my Friend and Encourager said, "When the Love of God takes up Its abode within the human heart, It sets in motion a force that is never stopped until Its full purpose is accomplished." I thought about this for a while. Then He added, "The mills of God DO grind slowly, but they DO grind exceedingly well." I have seen miracles happen in that life since that time. The faithful promise has come to me from time to time for myself as well as others.

SONG TO JESUS

It had been a long and weary morning. I lay down to rest and talk to the Lord about the situations at hand. I was sinking off into sleep, when suddenly this song began to sing itself within me.

You have given me love, You have given me joy,
You've given me comfort, Without alloy.
You've given me beauty, With a glorious hue,
But best thing of all, You have given me You.

You have given me hope, Took away my despair;
When the way has been dark, I've known You right there.
You've given me faith, Expectancy, too,
But best thing of all, You have given me You.

You've given me meekness, Took away my vain pride,
You've given me refuge, A sure place to hide.
You've taken the clouds, Leaving my sky all blue,
But best thing of all, You have given me You.

You've given me wisdom, You've given me light,
You've given me sunshine, To scatter my night.
You've given repentance, Your mercy to sue,
But best thing of all, You have given me You.

You've given a language, To sing forth Your praise,
You've given me mercy, To last all my days.
You've given me glimpses, Of Heavenly view,
But best thing of all, You have given me You.

You've given me truth, And the will to declare
Your glory and honor, Proclaim everywhere.
You've given Your spirit, And great good gifts, too,
But best thing of all, You have given me You.

I'm going to Heaven, Be there evermore.
I'll shout Hallelujah, My spirit will soar.
I'll see all my family, My loving friends, too,
But best thing of all, I will be there with You.

I'll praise You forever, I'll sing of Your grace,
I'll mount up in rapture, When I look on Your face.
I'll then love You truly, I'll worship You, too,
And thank You forever, For giving me You.

My Friend and I walked down a path along a shaded stream. We were barefoot. We came to the water's edge. We waded in and walked up a little way. The rocks on the bottom felt hard but smooth to my bare feet. The water ran over them cool and soothing. We stopped. I looked down at my feet — and His; at the flowing clear water and the smooth hard rocks. I looked up into His face. He was looking at me tenderly. He smiled. The vision was ended. His Presence and His Peace remained.

The next day an earthly friend and I drove in strange country. We turned down a road into a shaded area. My friend stopped the car. We got out. It all seemed so familiar. I had never been there, yet I knew I had. There was the path leading to the stream! I took off my shoes. This was holy ground! I walked into the water. I felt the rocks smooth and hard to my bare feet. The water ran cool and clear over between the two. We are a citizen of both Heaven and earth, Light and darkness, Love and hate, Faith and fear, Peace and war, Tranquility and confusion, Happiness and misery. They are the Inner Heaven and the outer darkness. One day we shall no more go back and forth. We shall only go forth. No more shall we be a stranger in a strange place searching for our own city. We shall have found our permanent dwelling place and be forevermore at home.

I was going on a journey. Several courses were available to me. My family and friends were trying to make it easy for me. They'd take me to the plane or to the train. Both were quite a distance away. The local bus was slow and left late in the afternoon. I'd have to make two changes.

I lay sleepless trying to decide. I wondered if I should go at all. From sheer exhaustion I fell asleep. When I awoke, my Guide and Counselor was saying, "My ways are always the simple ways." I believed. Relief and joyful expectation came. Of course, I was to take the local bus! Why had I ever considered otherwise? The trip was delightful. I was moving, with conscious direction from God.

THREE SIDES TO EVERY STORY

The wife of a young man very dear to me was complaining against him. I was troubled. Thinking about this I thought, "That is her side. I have not heard his. There are two sides to every story." My Teacher corrected me. He said, "Three. Hers. His. And Mine." Then I knew that God was working out His purpose in their lives and mine. Now the young wife doesn't complain about her husband. God's side has prevailed for her. I no longer think bad thoughts about the young wife. God's side has prevailed for me, also.

EVERYTHING'S ALL RIGHT

I saw in a night vision a soft, white, glowing, transparent substance. This substance surrounded and filled all things everywhere. I knew it was the Essence of God — His abiding presence. I thought, in the dream, "Nothing can ever really hurt us. We are really indestructible."

The scene changed. I saw a little boy and girl. They were troubled about a situation in the family. Finally the little boy said, "I'm going to bed. Everything's all right." The little girl looked at me. Her eyes asked, "Is it really?" I smiled and nodded. They went into the next room and shut the door. I waited a minute and opened the door. It was dark inside. A shaft of light entered the room. I saw the little girl prepared for bed. She danced around. Her curly pigtails danced up and down. She sang a lilting tune. The words were, "Everything's all right. Everything's all right. Everything's all right."

Often I think of the protecting cover of God's Light. Often I think of the little boy's faith. Often I think of the little girl singing in the dark, "Everything's all right. Everything's all right."

I saw a Father and His child upon a road. The child was about three. The Father held the hand of the child. They walked slowly on. The child didn't want to go. The child was kicking, screaming and dragging his feet. The Father walked on undisturbed. He took the rebellious child with Him.

Days passed. I again saw the Father and child. They were on the same road. The Father had released the hand of the child, but He kept His eye on him. The child was now perhaps twelve. He was in a hurry. He ran on ahead. The Father walked calmly at an even pace. The child was running more slowly. He was hot, tired and sweaty. The Father caught up with him. He took his hand. They arrived at the same place at the same time.

More days passed. Again I saw the Father and child on the road. The child was now a young man. He was walking tall and strong by his Father's side. They were conversing. Now and then they would laugh together. The child had grown to maturity. He was no more rebelling at the Path of Life. Neither was he hurried, worried or distressed. He had learned to trust his Father. They were friends. He walked with God.

ALWAYS SAFE AT HOME

I was far away from home, among strangers. A feeling of fear came upon me. Then my Comforter and Friend was saying to me, "You are in the same place now that you are when you are safe at home in your own bed. YOU ARE IN ME." Fear fled. I was released to have a wonderful time among new friends. Our True mutual Friend had made it so. He is in us, we are in Him; we are always safe at home.

We had bought a small trailer and were to move out of our big house. That night I could only think of a multitude of reasons why we shouldn't have done it. I saw impossible obstacles before us. Suddenly, my wonderful Counselor was saying, "The dark places will be made light AS YOU COME TO THEM." Then I saw this familiar road I know as the Path of Life. I looked down it. I saw dark shadowy spots. I knew the evil spirits of doubts, fear and mistrust lurked there. I looked down at my feet. There, it was light and sunshiny with beams of light shining down from above. I knew I was not to look *down* the road. I was only to look at the bright light right at hand. Thus I would ever walk in the light.

HOPES

I saw a winding path. It went upward around a hill. It was paved with stones. The stones were smooth, flat and white — like marble. They were placed far apart — so far apart you could not step from one to the next. Between the stones was mud. The Voice of my Teacher was saying to me, "The path is the Path of Life. The stones are 'hopes.'" He was silent for a moment. He added, "The same rain that washed the mud off the stones also washed it between them."

I knew at the top of the path would be all solid stone — a sure and steadfast hope.

INEXPRESSIBLE GRACE

I was talking with a friend. He said, "Sister, you exaggerate the Grace of God." His words rang in my ears. The day passed and the night came. On my bed I said, "Lord, do I exaggerate Your Grace?" No answer came, but I slept sweetly and soundly. When morning came, my Teacher was saying, "The Grace of God cannot even be expressed. How can it be exaggerated?" I had my answer. I continue to grow in Grace. It can never be exhausted.